CW00458319

HOPE LIVES BETWEEN US

HOPE
LIVES
BETWEEN
US

How Interdependence Improves
Your Life and Our World

JOHN R.
KIRKSEY

HOUNDSTOOTH
PRESS

HOPE LIVES BETWEEN US

How Interdependence Improves Your Life and Our World

FIRST EDITION

ISBN   978-1-5445-3716-0 *Hardcover*

978-1-5445-3717-7 *Paperback*

978-1-5445-3718-4 *Ebook*

This book is dedicated to my clan:

Helen Germaine Kirksey

Dayn and Meghan Kirksey

Elijah, Amara, and Michaiah Kirksey

Roy and Maggie Kirksey

Marilyn Kirksey Moore

Janice Kirksey Croft

Howard and Marian Calhoun

Derrick Calhoun

And all eight billion clan members

CONTENTS

FOREWORD

Foreign Policy Association Fellow John Roy Kirksey attributes to Leo Tolstoy the observation that "everyone thinks of changing the world, but no one thinks of changing himself." Kirksey is an exception to this observation, for he is the rare individual who embraces personal and political transformation. In this inspiring book, he exhorts us to be our best selves. He invokes George Eliot: "It is never too late to be what you might have been." I would submit that the same can be said for whole societies and for nation-states.

There are those who posit that America is growing apart, possibly permanently. They have not read John Kirksey's book. Kirksey's expansive and inclusive vision is key to the success of a diverse democracy like the United States. Kirksey demonstrates how important it is to build understanding through dialogue and patient engagement. In Kirksey's words: "This book is not a formulaic paint-by-the-numbers exercise on how to be more fully connected. It is instead meant to stimulate us to explore those dimensions of ourselves and of others that we may not have discovered, considered, or valued. It is only together in harmonious interdependent community that any one of us will become whole." Hence, the subtitle of this book: "How Interdependence Improves Your Life and Our World."

At a time when much of the world is beset by crises stemming from populism and xenophobia, Kirksey speaks to the promise and purpose of America. This is a book that seeks to lift the national spirit. For as former Yale University President Kingman Brewster Jr. observed, "A nation, like a person, needs to believe that it has a mission larger than itself." Indeed, Brewster, who also served as United States Ambassador to the Court of St. James, advocated for a Declaration of International Interdependence. Such a declaration would provide for "at least the beginning of global arrangements and institutions to safeguard the common defense and the general welfare of humanity everywhere."

Brewster elaborated in the pages of Foreign Affairs: "Then we would rediscover the sense of purpose, and once more know the satisfaction, of those who saved the peoples of the colonies by making them into a nation. We, in our turn, might save the peoples of nations by making them into a world community capable of survival."

There are generations that stand out for exerting a decisive influence on history. Speaking on the cusp of the Second World War, President Franklin Delano Roosevelt famously said, "This generation has a rendezvous with destiny." I believe that America today has a rendezvous with destiny but that we must first address frontally the growing domestic polarization that undermines our democracy and contributes to a corrosive lack of mutual respect.

I think it is noteworthy that we rarely, if ever, hear disrespectful discourse at Foreign Policy Association meetings. Yet far too much of the debate about the future of diverse democracies consists of attempts to ridicule or vilify rather than to engage or persuade. Instead of denouncing others, we need to enter into a real debate about the kind of future we seek to shape. I am pleased that this is one of the aims of the Foreign Policy Association's Great Decisions Discussion Program. Recently, I spoke with a librarian at the Kanawha County Public Library in Charleston, West Virginia, which sponsors a Great Decisions group. The librarian told me that the participants, while seriously engaged in their discussions, do so constructively and with an eagerness to hear the opinions of others. Great Decisions participants live up to Mary Catherine Bateson's observation that "we are not what we know but what we are willing to learn."

In the age of globalization, we must replace the valor of ignorance with the valor of learning if we are to succeed in an increasingly competitive world. Michael Mazarr, a senior political scientist at the Rand Corporation, wrote, "In the struggle for advantage among world powers, it is not military or economic might that makes the crucial difference but the fundamental qualities of a society: the characteristics of a nation that generate economic productivity, technological innovation, social cohesion, and national will."

Mazarr noted that most competitive societies "place a strong social emphasis on learning and adaptation. They are fired by the urge to create, explore, and learn. Instead of being shackled by orthodoxy and tradition, they embrace adaptation and experimentation and are open to innovations in public policy, business models, military concepts and doctrines, and art and culture."

As with the author of this book, Mazarr stresses the benefits of a melting-pot society. He stated that "most dynamic and competitive nations embody a significant degree of diversity and pluralism. A broad range of experiences and perspectives helps generate more ideas and talents that in turn sustain national power."

Why then is America so polarized? In his thought-provoking book, *The Great Experiment: Why Diverse Democracies Fall*

Apart and How They Can Endure, Yascha Mounk argues that "the rise of populist politicians who denounce their opponents as corrupt or illegitimate is the most important proximate cause to the new era of polarization." Efforts to delegitimize the opposition are tantamount to avoiding a democratic contest and to winning by default. Consequently, the electorate is deprived of the benefit of a proper ventilation of the issues.

In his excellent book *Lincoln and the Fight for Peace*, John Avlon stresses the importance of Lincoln's reconciling leadership style that seeks to unify rather than to divide. The importance of good leadership cannot be overstated in meeting both domestic and global challenges. While great leaders are critical to a nation's destiny, an enlightened public is also necessary, which is why great leaders are great teachers. Eleanor Roosevelt, an early supporter of the Foreign Policy Association, remarked, "You cannot be a great leader unless the people are great."

Civil society also has a role to play in shoring up a consensus on the importance of civil discourse to a vibrant democracy. Indeed, civil discourse is a civic responsibility, and an informed public is the best antidote to those who seek to poison our democracy with disinformation.

Facts underpin democratic processes. *New York Times* columnist Michiko Kakutani observed, "Without reliable information, citizens cannot make informed decisions about the issues of the day, and we cannot hold politicians to account. Without commonly agreed upon facts, we cannot have reasoned debates with other voters and instead become susceptible to the fearmongering of demagogues. When politicians constantly lie, overwhelming and exhausting us while insinuating that everyone is dishonest and corrupt, the danger is that we grow so weary and cynical that we withdraw from civic engagement. And if we fail to engage in the political process—or reflexively support the individual from our party while reflexively dismissing the views of others—then we are abdicating common sense and our responsibility as citizens."

Sadly, many overlook the responsibilities of citizenship in a democracy. Yascha Mounk wrote, "As citizens of democratic countries, we do, collectively, hold a lot of political power—and have a corresponding obligation to make our voices heard in moments of crisis. It's incumbent on us to vote for parties that are committed to making the great experiment succeed, to advocate for policies that would realize the promise of diverse democracy, and of course to protest when governments target minorities or deepen discrimination." In the current environment, the irrational backlash against Asian Americans due to the Covid pandemic that originated in China must be condemned in the strongest terms.

At the 2022 Foreign Policy Association Annual Dinner, Dr. Ashish Jha, White House Coordinator for the Coronavirus Response, asked for the most important word in times of pandemic. The high school teachers participating in the Judith Biggs Great Decisions Teacher Institute immediately gave the correct answer: trust. In my closing remarks at FPA's Annual Dinner, I underscored the importance of three more words that capture FPA's mission: truth, knowledge, and vision. These are more likely to prevail where education is valued and perceived as a high calling. Therefore, we must renew our commitment to educating our fellow citizens. Without a capacity for critical thinking, the revolution in social media presents a minefield that bodes ill for our collective future. H.G. Wells put it succinctly: "Civilization is in a race between education and catastrophe."

Noel V. Lateef
President, Foreign Policy Association
July 4, 2022

PREFACE

"Yesterday I was clever, so I wanted to change the world. Today I am wise, so I am changing myself."

—RUMI

I was born in the primarily working-class city of Rockford, Illinois. Rockford has a population of around 150,000 and is the fifth-largest city in Illinois. But my hometown had a distinctly small-town vibe, with many of the customs and ideas often associated with small towns. Racism, xenophobia, homophobia, and chauvinism, though not prevalent, were not unknown. All these -isms and phobias stemmed from unwillingness to know or engage with others who were perceived as different.

Growing up, I was always surrounded by grandparents, aunts, uncles, and countless cousins. There was love, familiarity, and security, yet I knew I had to get out and discover more about who I was. Upon graduating from high school, I moved to Chicago to attend college. Though Rockford was only ninety miles away, my grandmother was horrified, and her horror was only heightened when a few months later, another of her grandsons, my cousin Jimmy, moved to Chicago to join me.

Jimmy and I broke out in ways other members of our family had not, and to this day we reminisce about how our lives were transformed by our decision to leave our hometown. We did not abandon our family lessons of love, sharing, and learning. But we opened ourselves to an expansive richness of experiences with others who might express those same values of love, sharing, and learning as filtered through their own cultural experiences and messages.

As I began to more fully appreciate that my way was not the only way, I considered and often incorporated other ways. It quickly became clear that my way was merely one of many ways to view the world. And my way was not necessarily the best way. As I considered perspectives and ways that differed from my own, I often found that neither my way nor the other's way was better, nor the best. But I saw that through diligent discussion, debate, and analysis of differing ways, people could arrive at a better way.

When I first moved to Chicago, I lived with my father's

brother and his family for several months. Two young men who were a couple of years older than me lived next door. We soon became friends. I visited with them often, listening to their great jazz collection, dining with them, and engaging in intellectually stimulating discussions. It was about a year later that my uncle told me the young men were a gay couple. This was an epiphany that changed my entire way of perceiving differences. I had gotten to know these young men as people who were friends—they were open and giving to someone who was open to them. Over the many years since, I have reflected on this experience as foundational to my understanding that the differences of others are merely puzzle pieces in the oneness of which I am a part.

It did not take long for me to begin my exploration of interdependence and discover that my life was but a thread in a much greater tapestry. Friends and classmates became like a new kind of family to me. My best friend was, like me, named John. We met at the start of our first day on campus as we were trying to navigate our new environment. When my best friend's mother invited me to the dinner table, there was an unspoken understanding that her son and I made us each better than either would have been alone. A couple of years later, my friend John introduced me to Helen, one of his childhood friends. Helen and I have now been married for over fifty years. When you cast a stone into the stream, it changes the course of the stream forever.

Soon I entered the world of work. It was here that my true exploration of my place in the world began. Almost immediately, I began to realize that I possessed an innate ability to grasp the dynamics of human behavior in organizations. This interest and ability naturally led me into a long career in human resources, change management, and cultural dynamics. It has been a long and fascinating journey of enlightenment and exploration that morphed from observing and analyzing the actions and interactions of others. It became clear to me that having a true understanding of others required me to develop a fuller understanding of myself. This awakening led me to an exploration of self: my actions and interactions, my assumptions, and my values. It was not long before it became abundantly clear that my wish for a better world hinged on becoming a better me. It also occurred to me that my world would only become better if I did all in my power to make the lives of others better.

My long career has been a colorful journey. My life has been a vibrant kaleidoscope, constantly transforming me through my many interactions with so many others. My career allowed me to travel the world, observing, incorporating, and embracing the ways of other people and other cultures. I have learned that the world is not something apart from me but an indelible part of me. I am a part of everyone, and everyone is a part of me.

CHAPTER 1

———

WE CAN BE BETTER

"You must not lose faith in humanity. Humanity is an ocean; if a few drops of the ocean are dirty, the ocean does not become dirty."

—MAHATMA GANDHI

I envisioned this book as a universal exposition of my observations on the potential for our human community to live in harmonious accord. This vision was driven by my unwavering belief that there are universal truths that can guide us to a more perfect world. Underpinning my conviction is the inescapable truth that we are all inextricably bound in interdependence with all others.

I know that human beings have never been perfect, nor will we ever be. The very nature of our humanity renders us fallible. We make mistakes, and we are prone to err. We slip and fall. But we can always rise. Though we cannot reach perfection, we can always be better. We can learn from our mistakes and the mistakes of others. We can take lessons from the mistakes of history. We are often told that history is destined to repeat itself, but we are not bound to continually fall down the same rabbit holes. When I ceased to envision myself as one and began to embrace my connection to the oneness of the cosmos, I realized that I could and would be better.

Human evolution is not limited to our physical and mental lives. These aspects exist as just two of the dimensions of our tripartite being. Spiritual and emotional evolution is the third, and it is perhaps the ultimate challenge to the fullness of our being. It is our spiritual dimension that ties us to our oneness with the human community. And I am greatly encouraged by the fact that I have recently been witness to a remarkable awakening to the light of our oneness. People from the LGBTQ community have been elected and appointed to national state and local government leadership positions. People of color are ascending the corporate ladder in previously unheard-of numbers. Global leaders are becoming more acutely aware that their destinies are tied together by economics, climate control, health issues, and the constant ebb and flow of people, whether emigrating or traveling for business and pleasure. More and more, the world is waking up to the fact that it's good to be multilingual, that electric cars are good and inevitable, and that there are mixed-race couples whose biracial children eat Cheerios.

Am I saying that we are fully engaged on the journey to a brighter and more sustainable human community? By no means am I so naïve as to suggest that we have arrived. But the signs are clear that we are taking early and tentative steps. We must resolve to not retreat. We must move ahead with the understanding that any worthwhile endeavor will encounter countervailing forces. Newton's third law of physics states that "for every action, there is an equal and opposite reaction." Whenever we move toward the positive, negative forces will attempt to push back. But those opposing forces can only prevail if we are not resolute in our forward movement. In fact, if we do not encounter those countervailing forces, we may not be going in the direction we need to. Sometimes, obstacles are not placed in our path to stop us but to test us. Obstacles are challenges to face and overcome.

But we must be prepared for this journey and the inevitable obstacles we will encounter. If, as part of your physical fitness regimen, you prepare to embark on a hiking trail through rugged foothills, you do not don your bedroom slippers. No, you lace up in the best pair of sturdy hiking boots that you can find. Why? Because you know that you will be encountering uneven terrain and rocky paths that require the appropriate gear. You want to embark on this spiritual trek with your emotional gear firmly in place.

This book is about us. It is about the realization that we

can be better, and we must be better. It is about our inter-connectedness and the unrealized personal potential we all have. I stress to you that this is nothing new. These ideas have been with us for thousands of years; I am merely passing on borrowed wisdom from a vast repository of history and philosophical thought. The age-old visions for a better world, whether from Confucius, Marcus Aurelius, John Donne, Thomas Paine, Chief Seattle, Rosa Parks, Mahatma Gandhi, Mother Teresa, Dr. Martin Luther King, or Anne Frank, all tell us that we are, each and every one of us, connected one to the other. As John Donne wrote over four hundred years ago, "Ask not for whom the bell tolls. It tolls for thee."

The bottom line is that there is no me without you and no you without me. None of us will be whole until we realize that we are not independent of others, and we are not dependent on others, but we are ineradicably *interdependent*, one with the other. If we wish to survive and flourish as a species, we must acknowledge, embrace, and make manifest our human interdependence. *E Pluribus Unum* is the Latin inscription on the Great Seal of the United States. It translates as "Out of many, one." This inscription signifies an amalgam, a mixture or blend of all our precious uniqueness and individuality in pursuit of the common good. *Out of many, one* is a clarion call for unity. It is a challenge to value, embrace, and leverage the novelty of our differences for the benefit of all.

But to fully appreciate the phrase *E Pluribus Unum*, we can consider its genesis in Cicero's paraphrase of the philosopher Pythagoras: "When each person loves the other as much as himself, it makes one out of many."

We are all unique fragments of the one, and none of us can be whole until all of us are whole.

If many have recognized this human interdependence for millennia, why have we not acted in a manner that is beneficial and even essential to every one of us? Is it because we do not want to be better? Or is it perhaps because we are hoping that all will just get better?

It seems to me that most of us spend a great deal of time and energy wishing that the world was a more perfect place, with more perfect people. But few of us appear to see that we are, each of us individually and all of us collectively, the key to fulfilling our most sincere wish for a more perfect world. It starts with us—with me and you.

Though our wish for human perfection may be sincere, we miss two critical truths. The first is that we are not perfect. The second is that while our basic nature as human beings precludes any one of us from ever being perfect, we can all be better. And in being better, we bring ourselves and the world closer to perfection. Even though we are destined to fall short of perfection, we are meant to become better. We are destined to play our unique roles in making a more perfect world. The legendary author of the classic novel *War and Peace*, Leo Tolstoy, said, "Everyone thinks of changing the world, but no one thinks of changing himself."

Let's stop waiting for the world to get better. Let's look to ourselves to make it better. Why not start by examining what has made us who we are? I wrote earlier about some of the things that I experienced during my life, and I briefly talked about how those experiences became messages about the world and how I fit into that world. That was a brief synopsis of the many messages that I have gotten about not only who I am but also about who others are. In order for us to grow into better and more complete human beings, each of us must reflect on and challenge all the messages that we have internalized as our own about ourselves and others. I made a conscious decision that I would not live my life in fear or anger or hate. I knew that the way for me was to strive for a world where harmonic relationships prevail. To do that, I had to challenge myself to question and question and question who I was. I knew that I must become better. We must all become better.

Let's begin by thinking of ourselves as analogous to a computer's hardware. We can think of all the messages that we receive and accept about ourselves and others as the software that has been written for our hardware. Some of those software messages are taught to us over the course of time. For example, most of our parents taught us to be careful around hot surfaces because they can burn us. They may have said, "Don't go into the deep end of the pool because you don't know how to swim." Those were practical survival messages from people who loved us and wished to keep us safe.

But there are also many lessons that were caught and not taught. Some of those messages came from those same loving parents—for example, when you drove through a neighborhood of people who looked different or spoke a different language and the car windows were rolled up and doors got locked. Did your parents intend to teach you that those other people were bad and dangerous? Was their intent to instill fear, dislike, or mistrust of others? Perhaps not. Perhaps their operating hardware unconsciously obeyed its embedded software commands. They could say in good conscience that they did not *explicitly* teach you to fear those who are not like you. But do you see what has been done to us, intentionally and unintentionally? We absorb all these intentional and often unintentional messages about the world around us, about us, and about others, as well as about how we should interact within this confusing and often contradictory milieu.

As I just illustrated, some messages come from parents. But other powerfully imprinted messages come from other family members, schools, religious institutions, media, peers, and personal experience. Think back to some of the messages you have gotten. Messages about others as fixed standards are stereotypes. It is easy to apply stereotypes to an entire group of people who are different from us, or even to those who *are* like us. And it is especially easy if we observe someone from another group who happens to fit our adopted stereotype. If you visit a pub or bar where you observe a person or perhaps persons of Irish descent who are drunk, it becomes easier for you to access and validate the part of your software that has been programmed to believe that Irish people are boozers. But if you challenge that stereotype, you might immediately realize that you have Irish acquaintances who either drink little or do not drink at all. The same might hold true for you if you see on television that someone is mugged by a Hispanic or Black individual or group. But upon reflection, you know that your own Hispanic and Black acquaintances are upstanding and law-abiding citizens.

But as often happens, you may not have Irish or Hispanic or Black or White or gay acquaintances. So those unchallenged stereotypes about individuals in those groups are reinforced and likely passed on to others. You have failed to see the individual outside of your programmed stereotype for their group. You have forfeited the opportunity to observe and perhaps benefit from the other's individual uniqueness, which could be the catalyst that makes the world a better and more perfect place.

Before we can make the world better, each of us must become better. The things that we have learned that stand in the way of positive interactions with others can be unlearned. We can rewrite the software. By upgrading our software, we upgrade ourselves.

Wow! What power can You 2.0 release into the world?

I have adopted a learning model in my work for many years. Understanding the learning process is helpful as we work toward a more connected and interdependent world.

The theory underlying this model was reportedly developed by Abraham Maslow but more likely was developed in 1969 by Martin M. Broadwell, who is President of the Center for Management Services and formerly taught management training at the prestigious Executive Management Institute of the University of Michigan. Broadwell entitled his model the "four levels of teaching." There are many learning models, but I prefer this one for its simplicity. It is easy to explain and easy to follow.

The model is commonly referred to as the Stair-Step model of the Hierarchy of Competence.

STAIR-STEP LEARNING MODEL

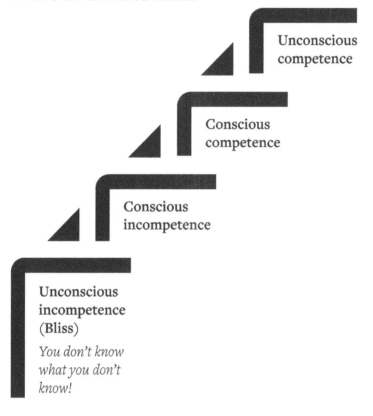

Unconscious
competence

Conscious
competence

Conscious
incompetence

Unconscious
incompetence
(Bliss)
*You don't know
what you don't
know!*

This model is based on competence development. The objective is to expand our cultural competence to become the best of ourselves that we can be.

The model begins with the premise that we are generally unaware of what we do not know. Simply put, you don't know what you don't know. Or, as we so often say, ignorance is bliss. This is the bottom step of the staircase and represents unconscious incompetence.

When you find yourself on this step, you are very comfortable because you don't know or comprehend the value of knowing something.

But sometimes you are hit over the head, figuratively speaking, with the realization that you don't know something that you really want or need to know. This automatically lands you on the second step, where you are now consciously incompetent. When you land on this step, the comfort factor disappears.

The second step is critical because it is a decision point. You do not automatically move to the third or fourth steps. At the second step, where you now know what you do not know, you can choose to remain there in perpetual angst or commit to learning what you do not know. Step one is a comfortable place because it allows you to remain blissfully ignorant. In step two, the bliss is replaced by the choice to remain uncomfortable in knowing that you do not know something that you want or need to know or to acquire the knowledge.

If you make the decision to learn what you do not know, you will begin the journey to step three: conscious competence. Getting to step three requires you to put in work. You must strive to acquire knowledge, and you must practice the application of that newly acquired knowledge. It won't be easy because on this step, you are aware that you are doing something that feels unnatural. It is not yet second nature. But if at step three you remain diligent in practicing application of your newfound learning, there will come a point where you automatically land on the fourth step of unconscious competence.

On step number four, you are on autopilot. What was once new and perhaps perplexing has now become programmed into your software so that you apply the new behaviors without even thinking about it. You are becoming a new and better you: You 2.0.

Here is an example of how this works. When I was about sixteen or seventeen years old, my father owned a little Chevy Corvair. I was a newly licensed driver, and I was thrilled that I might get to drive that sweet sporty car. The car had a four-speed manual transmission. At the time, I had been driving on a learner's permit for a couple of years and was accustomed to driving cars with automatic transmissions.

For those of you who have never driven a stick shift car, I will tell you that it is not in the least bit intuitive. In a car with an automatic transmission, you turn on the engine, shift into gear, and drive. The automatic transmission does all the shifting work. However, with a stick shift car, you start the engine, depress the clutch with your left foot, shift into first gear, and then gently increase the engine speed with the right foot while gradually releasing the clutch with the left foot. The car is now in forward motion.

But that's not all. When the car's gear reaches an optimal revolutions per minute (RPM) point, you must carefully repeat the clutching process to shift into second gear. Then, at the proper RPM, you repeat the process to shift into third gear. If the car is equipped with a four- or five-speed manual transmission, you shift again. At this point, you cruise along until you need to slow down or stop. When this occurs, you go into a complicated dance of depressing the clutch, downshifting to low gear, and slowing or stopping before beginning the process all over again. This rather laborious description is a prelude to the story of my adventure.

It all began one day when my dad was supposed to pick my mom up from work. This was before the days when every family had two or three cars (and furthermore, my mom never learned to drive). On this one particular day, my dad was feeling ill and asked me to take the car and pick my mom up from work. I was happy to do it. I would have a chance to drive that cute little car. As I noted, I was a seasoned driver in automatic shift cars. Plus, I had watched my dad drive the stick shift with apparent ease—and he had a prosthetic right leg. So how hard could it be for me to do it?

I was clearly on step one of our learning model, but neither my bliss nor my ignorance would last long. I began the struggle through my now conscious incompetence. The car reluctantly responded to my clumsy clutching and gear shifting with jerks and grinding sounds. I somehow managed the numerous stops and slowdowns, but I was woefully inadequate at using the clutch to manage my speed on the inclining streets in my hilly hometown. Somehow, I made it through this alien process to bring my mother safely home from work.

But, in the process, I burned out the clutch on my dad's new car and became painfully aware that I not only needed but desperately wanted to learn how to drive a stick shift car. I had come to step two of the competence ladder and was determined not to stay there. I am proud to report that, after long hours of conscious learning and practice, I did learn to drive a stick shift car, as long as I consciously followed the correct process. In this way, I was able to solidly stand on the third step of conscious competence.

I stayed on that third step for months, until one day I was running late for my summer job. I threw on my clothes, jumped in my car (I had bought a cheap used stick shift car of my own), and drove to work. I later realized that I had driven that car without consciously thinking about the process. I was on step four. I was unconsciously competent. Years later, while most of my driving is in automatic shift cars, I can still drive a stick shift without thinking about the process. My software was reprogrammed.

I am certain that you have your own story of climbing the learning steps. It may have been learning to ride a bike, play golf, play piano, or do algebra. The progression is the same. And we can apply the method to rewriting some of our software in ways that allow us to build symbiotic relationships with others.

While navigating new ways to envision yourself, you will hit speed bumps. As you develop competence in one dimension, you will discover that there are other messages that require challenging and rethinking. But if you just take a breath and continue forward, you will continue to move closer to the you that you want to be. My current automatic transmission car, unlike cars of yesteryear that required you to put a key into the ignition and turn, requires me to have the key on my person, press the brake pedal, and push an ignition button on the dashboard. Then, after putting the car into gear, I must depress a small lever that releases the emergency brake prior to driving. These are all wonderful new innovations for convenience and safety that have nevertheless required me to reprogram my software.

A manager at one of the major financial organizations in New York City told me a story that has stuck with me. This young woman had grown up in a suburban Midwest town with little ethnic or racial diversity. She related to her peer managers that her father was extremely prejudiced and lectured her regularly on the dangers of people who looked different from her. She said that she found his messages so outrageous and offensive that she made a conscious decision to move to New York City, where she could be involved in a diverse cosmopolitan community. She was surprised and disheartened to realize that sometimes when she was riding on a crowded subway, her father's message reel of bigotry and intolerance would run in her head. Shocked, confused, and revolted, she realized that somehow those messages had been programmed into her subconscious, and she became determined to reprogram her software with her own narrative.

We not only internalize stereotypes of others, but we also adopt and internalize societal stereotypes about ourselves. Several years ago, I had an opportunity to be in the audience for an appearance by Archbishop Desmond Tutu, the world-renowned Nobel Peace Prize Laureate. Archbishop Tutu recounted how he had traveled from his native homeland of South Africa to a neighboring country to give a talk. Following his talk, he was driven to the small local airport, where he was scheduled on a flight back home. The portable boarding steps to the airplane were rolled into position for boarding as the plane's passenger door opened. As he began to ascend the steps, Archbishop Tutu observed the Black African pilot step out of the cockpit. He stopped dead in his tracks and wondered, *Does this man know how to fly this plane?*

Archbishop Tutu went on to say, "I immediately checked myself, boarded the plane, and experienced a safe and pleasant flight. But it dawned on me that I have gotten the same messages that others have gotten about people who look like me."

These messages are pervasive, and we are all susceptible to them. Even when we know that the messages are irrational and disruptive to our human community, they subconsciously register and become imprinted in our software. In order for us to become better and more fully human we must, as Archbishop Tutu did, challenge the stereotypes and reprogram ourselves.

Does experiencing these negative or bad messages make us bad people? No, it does not. But if we do not question and challenge these messages, they will doom us as individuals and relegate the whole of humanity to mediocrity. If we accept mediocrity and do not work to be better, the harm is to ourselves.

In the 1800s, Chief Seattle of the Suquamish Native American tribe wrote a letter to the president of the United States in which he stated, "This we know: the earth does not belong to man; man belongs to the earth. All things are connected like the blood that unites us all. Man did not weave the web of life; he is merely a strand in it. Whatever he does to the web, he does to himself."

It is abundantly clear that we need to challenge ourselves in order to move beyond self to others.

Four hundred years before the birth of Christ, Plato stated, "The unexamined life is not worth living." We must examine our lives. We must question and challenge until we become the best that we can be. Our spiritual evolution continues to lead us on the path toward unity and harmonious accord. Just as we crawled out of the primordial muck to physically evolve into modern human form, we will continue to climb until we reach a higher plane of evolution in our spiritual interconnectedness. Reprogramming allows us to become better people who can live interdependently in harmonious community.

So, who is this about? It is about us. It is about you and me. If we are waiting for someone else to change the world, we are lost. We are all infinitesimal parts of the one.

We will begin by getting to know ourselves and striving to become a better us.

Haile Selassie, former Emperor of Ethiopia, said, "We must become bigger than we have been, more courageous, greater in spirit, larger in outlook. We must become members of a new race, overcoming petty prejudice, owing our ultimate allegiance not to nations but to our fellow men within the human community."

Here I add my own observation that I am no one and I am nothing until I am a part of everyone and a part of everything.

We all have work to do, so let's get busy. We must continually seek that elusive goal of perfection in order to have better lives and a better world. We must seek to attain the unattainable. While we are on this journey, we need to keep in mind that individual perfection is an aspiration; it is not a destination.

We can begin by exploring perfection as a concept. The first definition for the word "perfect" in the Oxford Dictionary is "complete and not deficient." We mortals cannot be complete and without deficiency. But we can come closer to perfection by becoming one with the whole of humanity. Since we are each an essential part of that human whole, we can only approach individual perfection through perfection of the whole of humankind. And the whole of humankind cannot achieve perfection unless all of us collectively strive for harmonic accord (unity and balance) with the remainder of the whole. Only through our embrace of interdependence and oneness will the whole be unbroken and undiminished—and consequently perfect.

Therefore, though individuals cannot be perfect, the whole of humanity can achieve perfection. And perfection of the whole is dependent upon the symbiotic interactions of individuals. It follows that by becoming better, you are essential to the perfection of humanity. The very survival of our species and our world is dependent on you, me, and other imperfect individuals like us striving to be better by interacting harmonically with one another and with the whole of the natural world.

CHAPTER 2

___

CHOOSING INTERDEPENDENCE OVER INDIVIDUALISM

"Isn't everyone a part of everyone else?"

—BUDD SCHULBERG

Harmony is the blending of unique voices to produce a richer tone than any single voice is capable of producing. So, if our goal is to live together in harmonic community, where does that leave our devotion to rugged individualism? As a unique individual, why can't you be independent of others?

This deserves exploration.

I was born, raised, and acculturated in the United States

of America. Like almost all Americans, I grew up with the seemingly sacrosanct worship of individualism as an unquestioned cultural value. But if we step back for a moment and think about this deeply entrenched American cultural value, we may want to question how and why our software was programmed with messages about the value of individualism. What is the genesis of one of our culture's most closely held and fiercely defended cultural norms and values? And what does it mean for us in today's world?

Individualism is prized—even worshipped—in the United States as an admirable attribute of a true, red-blooded American. And few would dispute that this great country's early existence was dependent upon rugged individuals surviving an untamed, though bountiful, natural environment. But upon closer observation, we see that the underlying reason for this worship of individualism has, over time, been drastically altered.

Our world is very different from the world of our grandparents and their grandparents. For example, in 1776, the population of the United States of America was 2.5 million people. That is the current population of Houston or Phoenix. By 1890, the United States population was 76 million. Today the population of this vast country is around 330 million, with a projection of 420 million people by the year 2050. For every person in the United States in 1776, there will be 168 people in 2050.

Our sparse population of 1776 dictated that in a vast, wild, unknown continent, rugged individualism was of paramount importance for survival. You chopped your own trees from the surrounding forest while keeping constant watch for grizzly bears and mountain lions. Then you split the logs to use in building your rough-hewn log house. The remaining kindling provided the firewood for the crude hearth that provided heat in the brutally cold winter. The hearth doubled as your stove for preparing squirrel or rabbit and root vegetables that were stored in the root cellar you had painstakingly constructed a few yards from your cabin.

That same hearth was where you boiled water to sterilize the rags that you needed to assist in childbirth. Those rags were remnants of old clothing that you had hand-loomed and sewn. And many children were born to help in the hardscrabble farming of the rocky patches scraped from the earth after laboriously digging out the tree stumps that filled the small clearing around your one-room cabin.

You produced ten to twelve children, but with the sad knowledge that, with luck, five or six of those children would survive to help in the clearing, planting, and hunting that were essential to your family's bare level of subsistence. Some of your children died from malnutrition or a myriad of diseases resulting from the harsh living conditions and absence of medical care. Some other diseases stemmed from inadequate hygiene or exposure to the elements. That kind of life demanded rugged individualism—not for individualism's sake but for the sake of survival in an isolated and hostile natural environment.

Eventually you experienced increasing numbers of other pioneering settlers arriving. These new arrivals precipitated early efforts to establish settlements and communities. The settlements grew and began to ease the burden of your harsh independence and allow for greater *interdependence* through development of community. Someone built a sawmill to cut the boards into uniform sizes to make house-building easier. Someone else planted grain, which prompted someone else to set up a grain mill to grind the grain, which made food production easier. Someone else raised pigs, and another bred milk cows and chickens, and so on.

Families from the community gathered to help build one another's houses, barns, and stables. And then following the house or barn raising, the communal table was set out with all the meats, vegetables, pies, lemonade, and home-brewed beer as the community celebrated the validation of the common human bond. Doctors, storekeepers, and craftsmen began to provide services that further eased individual burdens. The crying need for individualism began to shift to mutualism.

But the software was programmed to recognize rugged

individualism as a virtue in and of itself rather than an obsolete necessity for survival. This worship of individualism eventually became memorialized as a cultural imperative that worked against mutualism. Individualism limits the individual, harms the greater good, and destroys the community. Isn't it long past time for a software update?

This discussion of the need to challenge obsolete cultural imperatives reminds me of a story one of my former consulting clients told me. His parents were descended from a family that survived the disastrous Donner party. In covered wagons, the Donner party set out from Missouri in the spring of 1846 with the intent to make the four- to six-month trek to California. But along the way, they became convinced that an alternative route was more direct. The Hastings Cutoff was promoted by a man named Lansford Hastings, who had never actually traveled the route himself. The Donner party decided to follow this new route.

But this new route was longer and far more treacherous than the established one. Following the Hastings Cutoff required the Donner party to cross the Sierra Nevada Mountain range. While a mere 100 miles from the Donner party's destination as the crow flies, this mountain range's height and proximity to the Pacific Ocean caused far greater snow accumulations than any other North American mountain range. As a result of the attempt to shorten their journey via this new and untested route, the Donner party became trapped by a high-country blizzard. They were marooned for months in ramshackle tents and lean-tos covered in several feet of snow. Many of the party died from starvation and exposure. Others resorted to cannibalism of the dead. The survivors, the majority of them children, struggled through the harshest conditions imaginable until the weather moderated and they were eventually rescued. One of the surviving children, Isabella Breen, lived until 1935.

My client stated that his ancestors' experience as survivors of the Donner party in those harsh and unforgiving conditions, with the total breakdown of community, had bred an amazingly strong ethos of individualism and self-sufficiency in his immediate family. While he was attending college, my client decided to test his parents' devotion to individualism by not calling home for an extended period of time in order to see if they would check on him. They did not. After six months of absolutely no contact, he finally gave in and called his parents. He did not relate this story with pride.

With a bit of reflection, we can see that such fanatical, unyielding devotion to rugged individualism will block our path to community and mute our collective consciousness.

And, while individual identity is a valuable feature of our personalities, we must apply that individual uniqueness toward the common good as opposed to self-centered egoism. The web of life is constructed of infinite unique individuals interlaced with all other unique individuals, creating an interdependent oneness.

The education guru Maria Montessori stated, "The purpose of life is to obey the hidden command which ensures harmony among all and creates an ever-better world. We are not created only to enjoy the world; we are created in order to evolve with the cosmos." Cosmos implies an orderly or harmonious universe. And harmony can only be achieved through the combination of parts in unity. Harmony is impossible to achieve alone.

We must find ways to shift our behaviors to achieve more symbiotic outcomes. If we can shift our thinking from the *right* way versus the *wrong* way, we may find a better way. In our modern world, with far more people, far less elbow room, and fewer boundaries, we must adapt to living our daily lives interacting with ever more people. Many of these other people are bringing with them increasingly greater cultural and individual variation. Embracing individual and cultural variation as essential to our interdependence will result in the harmonic community that brings all of us closer to the perfection that we seek.

Not only are we in increasing contact with others, but our backgrounds and experiences are becoming exponentially (more and more rapidly) varied. As we experience this increased exposure to other people's values and cultures, it is paramount to embrace the difference as not inherently good or bad but simply different. I cannot overstress this point. We fear what we don't know. We hate what we fear. And we want to destroy what we hate. Therefore, it is imperative that we strive to know and understand others. We must seek unity. Otherwise, we are bound for destruction of others and, by extension, destruction of ourselves.

I ask you to keep in mind that unity does not mean sameness. In fact, your uniqueness is the essential element in unity. In order to achieve unity, we must share our uniqueness with others and open ourselves to the uniqueness of others.

Father Thomas Merton, a midcentury American Trappist monk who believed that all religions lead to God and who wrote extensively not only on his own Christian beliefs but on Zen Buddhism, Confucianism, and Taoism, said, "We don't exist for ourselves alone, and it is only when we are fully convinced of this fact that we begin to love ourselves properly and thus also love others."

Our goal is not to change others but to embrace and incorporate those differences that bring us closer to full self-realization. Simultaneously, we must open ourselves up in ways that allow others to find reciprocal value in our uniqueness. Each of us is a small but uniquely essential part of the whole. And we must always interact in ways that enrich, expand, and nurture the whole.

This is far more self-consequential than we might imagine. If I stop worrying about me and focus on us and we, the way forward becomes less hazy, and the road signs are clearer. You and I (we) will come closer to perfection by joining with others in contributing to the perfection of the whole. When any one of us salutes the humanity of any other, it resonates like the vibrations of a musical instrument and strengthens our oneness with the whole of humanity.

The musician Doug Floyd said, "You don't get harmony when everybody sings the same note."

Over the course of many years, pursuing my interest in the complex nature and behavior of my fellow men and women, it has become increasingly evident to me that a seminal cause of disunity and dysfunction in our world is our fixation on the sanctity of cultural norms. This has led to the conclusion that "my way is the right way," and therefore, all other ways are the wrong ways. This sets up the "us versus them" system of division, disconcert, and discord. It shuts the door on meaningful discourse and dialogue.

If we believe that our way is the absolutely *right* way, it is inevitable that we will perceive any other way as the wrong way. But if we start with the premise that our way is *one* way, it leaves room for the possibility of another way, or even other ways. Through examination of our ways relative to other ways, we may even discover a new way that is superior to both our way and the ways of others. Become curious. Expand your world by exploring other people, other places, and the unexplored regions of self.

If I make no other impression in this book, I hope to impress upon you that your life and my life are not limited to you or to me. Our lives are unquestionably inclusive of you, me, and the vast remainder of humanity. We each exist as part of a far vaster whole. In order to fully realize ourselves, we must join our unique selves to the whole of humankind. How often have you told yourself, "I can't help it; this is just the way that I am. I have always been this way," or "This is the way it is done," or "This is the way it should be"? We all grow up with these beliefs we have been programmed to accept as absolutes—as immutable truths.

As I stated earlier, many of our beliefs are taught by our parents, our religious institutions, our schools, and our peers. But many are not taught but caught as we observe how those around us act, react, and, most importantly, interact. We tend not to question these supposed verities. We don't question our absolute truths because that would require us to question ourselves. After all, our beliefs are part of who we are as individuals. We often hold these beliefs with fanatical fervor. But if we don't question our beliefs, and consequently question ourselves, we will not grow.

We believe that invalidation of our beliefs, especially those that underpin our value systems, might invalidate us. But let's challenge that premise. We are not static beings that are unable to grow or adapt. We are dynamic life forces with expansive potential for learning and growth. Nothing that we have incorporated into our sense of self is immutable. We can reach outward, stretch our boundaries, and break our bonds. We are not locked into who we are or how we are. Our capacity for transformation is limitless. What has been programmed can be reprogrammed. If we are willing to explore the frontiers of our human potential, we can be better.

Deepak Chopra said, "Awakening is not changing who you are but discarding who you are not."

Personal perfection is an aspiration, not a destination. It is what we seek so that we, as individuals in harmonic accord with others, can perfect the whole of humanity.

We all learned early on that our ancient ancestors crawled out of the muck millions of years ago. From one primitive physical life form, over hundreds of millions of years, came simian primates who eventually walked on two legs and had articulated thumbs that allowed them to perform sophisticated tasks. They got busy making fire, crafting and working with tools, and inventing language. As our predecessors evolved physically, their brains also developed. Our magnificent brains provided the reasoning, envisioning, and planning capabilities required for us to become the dominant life form on earth. From the harnessing of fire to the invention of the wheel to automobiles and planes all the way to the laptop computer, smartphone, and wireless streaming, we evolved. I am composing on my laptop now. It is a far cry from the old word processor or electric typewriter or chiseling your thoughts onto a stone tablet. Amazingly, we have never ceased growing and evolving, both physically and mentally.

But are we limited to evolving on the bipartite dimensions of body and mind? There is a third dimension of human evolution that is too often viewed as static and immutable: spiritual evolution. When we consider body, mind, and spirit, it is essential to realize that evolution is central not only to body and mind but to all three dimensions of our tripartite existence. Humanity has arrived at a nexus where our evolution of body and mind will not be sustained without commensurate spiritual evolution. This spiritual dimension truly elevates humans above the lower life forms. Just as the articulated thumb makes humans unique among species, so does our capacity for spirituality.

At this point, I must add the caveat that our enhanced physical, mental, and spiritual evolution elevates us but does not separate us from all other life forms, whether fauna or flora. In fact, it invests us with a special responsibility as stewards of not only one another but of the earth that we inhabit.

In order for us to be complete, we must place spiritual evolution at the forefront of all our endeavors. By spiritual, I do not mean religious. You may or may not follow a religious creed. My reference to spirituality reflects the primary definition, as expressed in the Oxford Dictionary: "Of or concerning the spirit as opposed to matter." For you it may signify your adherence to Christianity, Judaism, Islam, Hinduism, Buddhism, or your beliefs about how to live life in harmony with humanity and nature.

A bit more than thirty years ago, my wife Helen and I relocated from Bucks County, Pennsylvania, to Miami, where I had accepted a new position. We had to acclimate ourselves to a very different cultural experience than the one we were accustomed to in the bucolic Bucks County. Miami is an exceptionally diverse amalgam of cultures, including many first-generation immigrants. The largest racial and ethnic population in Miami is by far White Hispanic, who comprise more than 60 percent of the population. The remainder of the population is African American non-Hispanic (13 percent), White non-Hispanic (13 percent), other Hispanic (4 percent), and African American Hispanic (2 percent). Adding to this mix is a religious community of Catholics, Protestants, Jews, Eastern Orthodox, and

Muslims. Completing this montage is a socioeconomic milieu with extreme and often flamboyant wealth set against a backdrop of abject poverty.

We might expect that this would be a thriving cultural crossroads for sharing experiences and viewpoints. We might expect a strong philanthropic community. We might expect Miami to be a model for what our world can be. Alas, this is not the case. I experienced Miami as a city of warring tribes, each clustered in their own little fiefdoms, daring others to intrude on theirs. And as far as the haves caring for the plight of the have-nots, Miami ranks ninetieth on the WalletHub list of Most Caring Cities of the hundred largest United States cities. In general, I found that others are not welcome in this city of others.

But there are always points of light. Within this seemingly unwelcoming city of Miami, I was reminded that I am the change I seek. As Helen and I began to immerse ourselves in our new business and civic activities, we established some of our most vibrant and enduring friendships. One such friendship, with two other couples, has endured and strengthened over time and distance. Did these friendships blossom due to our racial, ethnic, or religious similarities? No. My wife Helen and I are African American Protestants, while the other couples are White and Jewish. Both of the other couples are about ten years older than us. Our only obvious similarity was that we were all transplants to

Miami from the northeastern United States. But we met and immediately recognized a spiritual bond. Over the many intervening years, we have all found our lives enriched and enlightened as we have shared our authentic uniquenesses. I know that I have become a better me through my friendship with them. They have helped me to find my place as a small but essential piece in humanity's puzzle.

Helen and I recently attended a social gathering hosted by one of those couples. We are all living in the Northeast once more, in Bucks County; Greenwich, Connecticut; and Westchester, New York. We are just geographically distant enough from each other that we do not get together often enough. This only makes our reunions more precious and heartwarming.

During the event, we spent a good deal of time reminiscing about old times and how much we regretted not being together more often. During our conversation, one of the women and I attempted to explain what had brought us all together in such a strong, caring, and enduring friendship. It didn't take long for us to conclude that there was no easy explanation beyond an undeniable spiritual connection. Spirit is the seat of emotions and character. It is what makes us human. It is humanity's connective tissue.

In preparing this manuscript for this publication, I sought advice from a very dear friend, a deeply devout Christian minister who has authored several books. She was more than gracious in volunteering her time and energy to give me her valuable advice and perspective.

One suggestion from her was that when I discuss spirituality, I should consider discussing my own Christian faith. I wrestled with the idea for a few weeks. I usually do not discuss religion because it can become divisive, but I will approach this discussion on religion as a disruptor rather than a divider. While I am a Christian and have been since as early as I can remember, I do not follow my faith to the exclusion of other faiths or those who profess no religious attachment. I happened to have been born into a Christian family. And I believe that the basic tenets that I learned to value in my Christian religion are also the basic tenets of other major religious traditions. The respect for and valuing of human life and dignity, love for one's fellow human beings, human equality, and human charity are fundamental to most religious faiths. In fact, there are vast numbers of people who do not profess any religious faith but hold true to the basic tenets that underpin most religions. On the other hand, there are many who wrap themselves in the cloak of religion while ignoring the most basic religious tenets. Those who preach hatred, intolerance for differences, and denigration of other religions and who deny the basic dignity and humanity of others are not truly Christian, Muslim, Jewish, or any other religion that they may profess.

That is why when I honor my Christian religion, I honor the religions of all others. I also honor those who follow a path of love, charity, and peace while professing no religious affiliation. I speak of spirituality because I believe that it encompasses the oneness of which we are all a part and that embraces us all.

In my work as a cross-cultural consultant and advisor, there is an ethical principle often referred to as the platinum rule. That rule implores us to "do unto others as they would want to be done unto." Each of us is a uniquely different piece of humanity's puzzle, and what I need may be different than what you need. That is fine because my job is to become a better me while helping you to become a better you. What we all need is the loving embrace of the other.

When I was about seventeen years old, I was passionate about one day becoming a Christian minister. However, at some point, I became disillusioned by behaviors I observed in the church community. In fact, I was so shocked and disappointed that I withdrew from all religious activity for many years. I began to see organized religion as a sham, as fiction to control and manipulate the masses. I had heated debates with those who were firm and unquestioning believers. I went on like this until my early thirties.

One day, a young minister named Joe stopped by my house and invited me, Helen, and our young son to visit his church in our little suburban village. I was hesitant to accept his invitation. But I discussed it at length with my wife, and we eventually decided to try a visit.

That visit to Joe's church changed my entire perspective on religion. My wife and I began to refer to the church as the smiley face church because Reverend Joe wore a white smock with a big yellow smiley face on its front. That church, for me, represented the ideal for humanity. Even though Joe was a United Methodist minister, the church was nondenominational. There were Protestants, Catholics, Jews, Greek Orthodox, and others who all came together in love and community. I remember our church celebrating Greek Orthodox holy days and Jewish Seder. The congregation was White, Black, Asian, and Hispanic. There were wealthy people, poor people, and those from the middle class. Young and old came, not just from our village but from as far as thirty miles away, to be a part of this mini-utopia. Not only did this experience bring me back to religion, but it expanded my understanding of spirituality and community.

So, when I speak of spirit or spirituality, I am not excluding religion but embracing religion as one expression of our quest for oneness. Perhaps I am fulfilling my destiny as a minister. This work, this book is my ministry.

We often think of ongoing evolution as purely physical or

mental, as though spirituality is set and static. But spiritual evolution continues. Perhaps it is this spiritual dimension where we are just now becoming fully articulated. I believe we are on the cusp of a quantum leap in that evolution of spirit. I do not see a slow progression but a rapid advance in our spiritual awakening. It is essential to our wholeness and survival as humans that we each play a role in support of that inexorable transformation.

The Vietnamese Buddhist monk Thich Nhat Hanh wrote, "At any moment you have a choice that either leads you closer to your spirit or further away from it." It is incumbent on every one of us to make choices that elevate humanity. It is through continual nurturing of our individual and collective spiritual evolution that we will fully embrace our interdependence in pursuit of oneness.

Our spirit, as evidenced in our empathy, compassion, or joy in the well-being of others, is our path to becoming better—a better me, a better you, a better us, and a better world. It is our tether to the cosmos. Our way to harmonic community will be revealed as we expand our symbiotic relationships with others whose values, norms, and underlying experiences may be at variance from our own. We must set our path to encounter, embrace, and incorporate others. We will weave a richer, more vibrant, and more durable human fabric through the novelty that springs from our interactions with others.

If we begin to act toward a common good, if we seek harmony, we can live in a truly symbiotic state. We can discover a world where the whole is greater than the sum of the parts. Our aim should be for symbiotic coexistence.

The Oxford Dictionary defines "symbiosis" as "a mutually advantageous association or relationship between persons." This enables each person to be more than they could be without the other. Simply put, in symbiotic relationships, one plus one equals more than two.

Every interpersonal action should aim toward enhancing the well-being of *the other person or persons*, therefore enhancing the whole and, ultimately, enhancing your own well-being. Liberation of others is liberation of self.

As Dr. Martin Luther King said, "All men are caught in an inescapable network of mutuality."

CHAPTER 3

PUTTING VISION INTO ACTION

"If not me, who? If not now, when?"

—HILLEL THE ELDER

One example of how one individual, Sir Thomas Raffles, recognized interdependence as essential to the human community was unveiled to me when Helen and I recently visited Singapore—our second visit to that magical city-state. During our first visit, a bit over a year and a half earlier, the fabled Raffles Hotel was closed while undergoing a two-year renovation. We stayed across the street from Raffles in a perfectly lovely hotel.

We had an almost immediate feeling of belonging in Singapore and really wanted to return to spend time at the Raffles

Hotel. And so, Helen and I returned to spend a couple of weeks in Singapore, this time at the newly renovated Raffles Hotel. It was a truly transformative experience. For those two weeks, Helen and I were treated like family by the hotel's greeters, butlers, restaurant staff, hotel historian, and legendary Sikh doorman. The entire experience was one of welcoming community and harmonic resonance. Upon our departure, we were warmly and occasionally tearfully embraced by staff members who only two weeks before had been unaware of our existence.

Singapore and the Raffles Hotel are fabled settings of exotic possibilities. Founded 200 years ago on the southern tip of the Malay Peninsula, modern Singapore (called "the Lion City") was the visionary child of Sir Thomas Stamford Bingley Raffles, lieutenant governor of the Dutch East Indies. His ideal was to establish a truly multicultural community reflective of all inhabitants. The treaty founding Singapore was read aloud in all the languages native to the nationalities that were present, including English, Malay, and Chinese. Shortly after founding Singapore, Sir Thomas Raffles moved on to attend to his other colonial duties in the Dutch East Indies, leaving the administration of Singapore to British Resident William Farquhar.

Upon Lord Raffles's return in 1822, he observed that Farquhar's administration was grossly unsatisfactory. He saw that Farquhar was permitting vices such as gambling, opium dens, and slave trading to go unchecked in the young colony. This flew in the face of all that Sir Thomas Raffles had envisioned for his model colony. He knew that immediate reforms must be made.

With the assistance of the colony engineer, Lord Raffles immediately set about to draw up a master plan for Raffles Town.

The plan divided the city into four distinct areas. One area of town was designated for Chinese, one area for East Indians, one area for Malays and, of course, the best commercial area for Europeans. Despite the fact that the plan segregated the city by race, it was remarkably forward-looking for the day. In planning this city, Raffles exhibited an uncanny awareness that future progress would require more enlightened views of community. He established a Malay college that emphasized the importance of learning both native and European languages. He promoted fairness and morality, imposing heavy taxes on public drunkenness and opium smoking. He outlawed slavery. And he dictated that no criminal laws or prosecutions would be based on racial, ethnic, or religious principles. His efforts in this regard appear to have set the foundation for modern-day Singapore.

While not perfect, Raffles's vision set the stage for a robust Singaporean city-state that is now acknowledged as a thriving model of unity and interdependence. National Heritage Board Singapore wrote an article published in *National Geographic* that explained, "Cultural heritage is also reflected in Singapore's potpourri of festivals. The warm invitation extends to neighbors, friends, and family, regardless of race, language or religion. And no matter how different these celebrations may be, they all have distinct commonalities: reunions, traditional cuisine and well wishing."

Harmonic community embracing of the other is hallowed tradition in Singapore. Singaporean people of Chinese, Malay, Indian, and Eurasian descent continue to strive for more perfect and interdependent relations in this highly multicultural, multiethnic, and multilingual society. And since 1997, on July 1, they have celebrated Racial Harmony Day in honor of their success as a racially harmonious nation. The interdependent nature of the Singaporean state, as institutionalized by Sir Thomas Raffles, has made them a better nation that continues to become even better.

My fascination with the Singapore experiment stems from its existential affirmation of our human capacity to be better. If they can do it, so can we.

Singapore is a micro culture. It is a relatively small city-state, with a population of 5.8 million (compared to New York City's 8.5 million population). It is an experiment in harmonic community that has continued to thrive and evolve for more than two centuries. Though not perfect, it is a beacon on the road to perfection.

If we are to learn from and improve upon Lord Raffles's experiment in inclusive community, we must begin by asking: when should we begin this journey of self and human betterment? I believe we must start now from where we are and with whomever we encounter. We must strive for growth and improvement every second, every minute, every hour, and every day of our lives.

When faced with the necessity to improve ourselves, I will bet that you, like me, have often said, "I just don't have time," or "I will get around to it later." There is a German proverb that instructs: "Begin to weave and God will give you the thread." We must begin to weave. We can weave a rich tapestry of color and light reflective of our oneness with others. We can't wait! The time to act is now. Often that thin line between success and failure is hesitancy in execution. Eckhart Tolle wrote, "The only thing that is ultimately real about your journey is the step that you are taking at this moment."

Most cultural values and norms have arisen for sound and practical reasons. Once embedded in a populace, the values and norms tend to persist, even if the practical circumstances from which they sprang change or cease to exist altogether. I merely encourage an open and expanded vision and examination of the world so that we may see it through clearer lenses. When we see better, we can do better.

We are thinking and reasoning animals, with the ability to override our instinctive and immediate responses, as well as our resistance to ideas different from the ones we are accustomed to. In fact, if we step back long enough to acquaint ourselves with differences, and to seek value in those differences, we might discover new worlds. As our world evolves, we must also evolve by adjusting the lenses through which we view the world.

All world cultures and the coteries within arise from our basic need for survival. Our expression of those norms can be blatantly evident. I vividly remember many years ago being in Puerto Rico on my honeymoon. After a week or so of fun and free spending, I realized that my money was nearly gone. As any ruggedly independent newlywed would do, I decided to cable my father for additional funds. I found my way to the Western Union office in the central San Juan business district, where I planned to launch my plea to my dad. To my surprise and chagrin, I discovered that the office was closed for about three hours during siesta time. Siesta! I needed to get money *quick*. How dare they close in the middle of the business day? Upon inquiry, they explained that during the extreme tropical heat of the afternoon, it was next to impossible to keep the office open. But, in spite of feeling inconvenienced, I was greatly relieved to learn that the Western Union office reopened from the late afternoon into the evening.

Many years later, I was in Switzerland, in what is known as the "watch valley" that stretches from Geneva to Basel and is the cradle of the European timekeeping industry. I am an avid wristwatch collector, and I had planned on visiting some of the watch shops in Basel. I picked up a trolley schedule, bought a ticket, and went to the trolley stop nearest to my hotel. Not only was the train exactly on schedule, but my ticket was never collected. They ran on an honor system that assumed the discipline and honesty of passengers. Can you imagine that? I rode those trolleys many times over the following days and found the experience the same each time. The train was never late or early, always right on time. My ticket was never collected even though I always purchased one.

On the other hand, I have visited countries where time was malleable. Is one culture's way of viewing time right and the other wrong? No—neither is right or wrong. Just different. This is known as cultural relativism.

Claude Levi-Strauss, the French anthropologist and ethnologist, spoke of cultural relativism as follows: "Cultural relativism affirms that one culture has no absolute criteria for judging another culture as 'low' or 'noble.' However, every culture can and should apply such judgment to its own activities because its members are actors as well as observers." So, while we should not judge another culture, we should be vigilant in examining and questioning our own.

At the juncture of the differences between us and others lies novelty, which is the path to innovation and creativity. We often seek similar ends via different means. One example that I personally witnessed and participated in clearly demonstrates the power inherent in the novelty of divergent cultures collaborating symbiotically to create something more innovative, powerful, and better than either could achieve independently.

Two of the world's largest and most highly respected professional services firms realized that by merging into one rebranded firm, they had the potential to service clients even better. Fortunately, the merging firms realized that in order to leverage the potential of the combined firms, they would need to look beyond the traditional legal and financial due diligence involved in any business mergers and perform a thorough cultural due diligence. The firms contracted independent cross-cultural experts to perform an assessment of the two cultures to assess what might pose threats to the forthcoming merger.

The assessment revealed that the biggest difference in the cultures of the merging firms was in the way each approached projects. It was not that their end games differed—it was just that they traveled different paths to achieve identical goals. The cross-cultural expert defined this cultural dilemma very simply: "One firm is runners, and one firm is dancers." By running faster, you quickly reached the solution but may have caused some havoc along the way. On the other hand, while carefully choreographing your dance, you might sacrifice valuable time in executing the solution. The consultant's solution to this dilemma was simple and straightforward: "The dancers need to run faster, and the runners need to learn to dance." Simple yet profound.

This clear dilemma with its call to action prompted the firms to act quickly. About fifty of the firms' senior cultural and behavioral experts from a dozen or more countries convened in Brussels, where they spent a week brainstorming, modeling, and mapping scenarios for optimal performance of the newly combined cultures. The result was that they were able to create an action model that incorporated the best of both cultures and proved far more effective than that of either of the legacy firms. Twenty years later, the firm ranks among the world's seventy-five most valuable brands.

Once we establish that we seek the same end, we can compare and assess our different approaches to achieving that end. The results will most often lead us to novel approaches that far surpass what we could have achieved independently. This is the value of symbiotic (win-win) relationships. Simply stated, a cooperative relationship works to the advantage of all involved. The whole becomes greater than the sum of the parts.

This is similar to the phenomenon of adaptation in the plant world. The plant species that have proven most adaptable to living in symbiotic relationships with other life forms and have adapted to environmental change have not only survived but have thrived.

One of my main reasons for hesitation in writing this book is that the fundamental philosophies and life principles upon which I base this treatise are nothing new. Therefore, I have been telling myself that it is not only presumptuous but foolish to write about something that others over the centuries have sagely expounded on.

But, observing that we still struggle daily with our relationships and fail to value the well-being of others, I must assume that perhaps we don't believe that the well-being of others is important to our own well-being. Or, more likely, we are waiting for a guide to hand us a map that lays out how to live our lives more fully and interdependently with others.

If my latter assumption is correct and you are waiting for a guide, I have good news for you. The sages have spoken, and you can be the guide that you have been waiting for. You have within you the ability to harness and leverage the wisdom of those who have come before. I do not presume to teach you to live and act interdependently. But I do hope to facilitate your journey of discovery. You will change the world!

Why do I feel so deeply that you will change the world? It is because I am sensing a paradigm shift and because I see many people who know they need to embrace and cherish our oneness. We are redefining our tribal imperatives and realizing our tribe is the whole of humanity. I am witnessing a palpable hungering for the wholeness and harmonic accord that the wisdom of the ages has heralded.

The ancient—but always timeless—lessons on symbiotic living have largely been admired as intriguing philosophies or enchanting prose. But they are more than enchanting prose. They need to be embraced and treasured as rare and precious roadmaps to more productive human interactions. I am convinced that these lessons can serve as a practical working guide for those who want to play a part in creating a more perfect world where we live in unity and harmonic accord. We are at a juncture where we must decide whether we want to be a part of the march toward a better us and ultimately a better world. The alternative is unthinkable.

So, the question for me was: when do I leverage my

existence in service to the world? When do I cease being a spectator and take the field as a player and coach? The answer, loud and clear, was now. Not next month or next week, but now. Today. We don't require permission to be better.

In 1999, Willie Jolley wrote, "A vision without action is an illusion." I know that I waited a very long time before writing about my vision for a better us. But I know that I was meant to sing my song because it belongs not to me but to the world. I also sense that there is a readiness and indeed an eagerness and hunger for a life-affirming message of unity. Though it is my vision that I share with you, I believe that it will help you access your unique vision and embolden you to act now. I believe that you will be compelled to sing your own song in harmony with the greater oneness. The Victorian novelist George Eliot wrote, "It is never too late to be what you might have been."

So, abandon the would haves, the could haves, and the should haves—and replace them all with "I will now."

"The secret to getting ahead is getting started."

—MARK TWAIN

CHAPTER 4

CHANGE STARTS WITH YOU

"If I must start somewhere, right here and now is the best place imaginable."

—RICHELLE E. GOODRICH

Where do we start? This question is the most difficult part of any journey. But it can also be the most exciting step. I have learned that the best place to start is wherever you are. And you can start with whomever you encounter.

Personal experience is often an excellent guide in helping us to find the place to start our journey toward a more harmonious world. At one point in my career, I was the president of a nonprofit organization in Washington, DC. A few blocks away from my office there was a popular restaurant that had been closed for renovations for nearly a year. When the restaurant finally reopened, throngs of expectant customers eagerly flocked to pick up one of their favorite lunches. With the line stretching onto the sidewalk, I joined the crowd and hoped that I would be able to get served before my next afternoon meeting. I had been standing in line for about thirty minutes when a young man noticed my impatient fidgeting. He made eye contact, smiled, and gave me a nod of assurance. With that slight gesture, he reassured me that we were all in it together. It may not seem like much, but it was priceless. It reminded me of my place in the web of life. I do not know who he was and will likely never see him again. But in that brief and seemingly inconsequential encounter, he not only brightened my day but reminded me of our connection to the whole of humanity.

That young man unconsciously changed the world. He touched me in a way that changed not only my life but the lives of those of you who are reading this story. Knowing that positive inputs will result in positive outputs does not inform us of what those specific outputs will be. In my specific case, it helped to inspire this book. My retelling will likely inspire some reader's action, perhaps a smile or pat on the back, which makes our world a better place for us all. But we can be certain that sharing our unique selves is a vibrato within the web of life. The slightest touch of the web triggers a vibration that alters the course of all humanity.

Another of my chance encounters occurred a few years ago when I was shopping at a popular grocery store. Our area had recently been hammered by an exceptionally heavy winter snowstorm. The normally twenty-five-minute drive to this supermarket had taken me and my wife about forty-five minutes on treacherous ice-coated roads. The grocery store's parking lot had been partially plowed in order to clear lanes and parking spaces. But the plowing also produced three- to four-foot-high mounds of plowed snow between the parking lanes.

I had parked my car and was preparing to enter the grocery store when I noticed a woman whose car would not start. I inquired about the problem, and she tearfully related that her battery had failed, and she was unable to start her car. She was unable to contact an emergency service for assistance. As fortune would have it, I had battery jump-starting cables in my car's trunk. Without hesitation, I drove around the snowbank and positioned my car for the battery cables to reach hers. Within minutes, her car was running. She thanked me and was on soon her way. Again, I will likely not encounter her ever again.

But six months or so later, in far better summer weather, I was shopping in that same grocery store. After completing my shopping, I returned to my car, loaded my groceries, and made the twenty-five-minute drive back home. After putting my groceries away, I reached into my back pocket.

My wallet was not there. Panicked, I called the store to tell them that I had apparently lost my wallet. They asked for a description and then asked me to hold. After a few minutes, which seemed like hours, and as I was anticipating having to cancel my credit cards and get a new driver's license, they came back on the line and cheerily announced that someone had found my wallet and turned it in. I immediately drove back to the store. I was thrilled to find that everything was there, including six hundred dollars in cash. This was amazing, especially since I rarely carry more than ten to twenty dollars in cash. Again, my tether to the web of life was affirmed. It was as if my deed six months earlier had released reciprocity into the cosmos.

Cosmos is an intriguing word. Cosmos is often used interchangeably with universe. But cosmos is a much more nuanced word that modifies and expands the concept of universe. In the sixth century BC, the Greek philosopher Pythagoras defined cosmos as an "orderly and harmonious universe." Two centuries later, Plato described the cosmos as "a single living creature which encompasses all living creatures within it." We are all interconnected as unique and interdependent parts of the one inseparable whole—the cosmos.

I tell these stories because they demonstrate the nonlinear dynamics of human interconnectedness. In no way could I predict what my service to the woman whose car would not start might put out into our world. Would she be prompted to do something to ease the life of someone else? Could that someone else have done a good turn to the anonymous person who returned my wallet? I don't know, and I will never know. But I do know that what we release into the world changes the world.

No supercomputer has yet been able to predict the impact of nonlinear human interactions—nor will one likely be able to. But there is no action without a reaction. Simply put, the more good that we put out into the world, the more good we can expect from the world. Conversely, the more space that we open within ourselves for the reception of the good in others, the more abundantly the world will reward us all.

You may have heard of the butterfly effect, which showcases interconnectedness. The term was coined by mathematician and meteorologist Edward Norton Lorenz, best known as the founder of chaos theory, which focuses on the observance of systems that are extremely sensitive to initial conditions (any of a set of starting points). Simply stated, chaos theory posits that any active system, such as weather, can be unpredictably altered by even minute changes to the initial conditions.

In 1972, Lorenz presented a speech entitled "Does the Flap of a Butterfly's Wings in Brazil Set Off a Tornado in Texas?"

I am not a mathematician as Lorenz was, so I will not attempt a sophisticated explanation of his work. Instead, I will apply my understanding of what this work means for our human system dynamics. Although the butterfly does not directly cause a tornado, it contributes to the myriad other initial conditions that eventually create a tornado's path and intensity, or even whether it forms or not. Even the smallest input to a system will alter the output.

Human systems are also altered by even the smallest inputs. Several years ago, a study used the Standard and Poor's 500 Index to identify both the 100 corporations that were reputed to have the best record of incorporating diversity and inclusion (D&I) into their operations and the 100 corporations with the worst reputations for incorporating D&I. The results showed that the corporations with the best reputations for D&I experienced an annual return on investment (ROI) that was several percentage points higher than the group with the poor D&I reputations.

Some D&I practitioners began to assert this finding as proof that a strong D&I initiative drove enhanced ROI. I challenged this conclusion. My challenge was based on the fact that corporate diversity initiatives are not independent of all other corporate operations and initiatives. The corporations that have solid D&I programs tend to be corporations that are more advanced and innovative in most other operations and initiatives. Therefore, D&I initiatives complement all other corporate initiatives. D&I initiatives cannot be measured independent of other systems, only in combination with them. That is to say that if we do a combination of things well, including D&I, we can assume that is a winning combination if our ROI meets or exceeds expectations. We cannot impute the value of one of those inputs independent of the others. Dynamic systems always operate interdependently.

It is impossible to predict what intervening inputs will alter the course of our subsequent interactions. If I didn't get the proper sleep, my dog was sick this morning, or I got great news about my health or finances, any of those occurrences will impact how I interact with you or others I may come into contact with. Consequently, these interactions will influence how you and others relate to the rest of humanity. Following this daisy chain to its logical conclusion, we can see that the best course for all of us is to make our interactions as positive as possible. In this manner, we all become better, and humanity comes closer to perfection.

Four hundred years ago, John Donne wrote in his devotion, *For Whom the Bell Tolls*, that "no man is an island, entire of itself; every man is a piece of the continent, a part of the main; if a clod be washed away by the sea, Europe is the less, as well as if a promontory were, as well as if a manor of thy friends or of thy own were; any man's death diminishes me, and therefore never send to ask for whom the bell tolls; it tolls for thee."

What a powerful allegory for our interdependence. Whatever we do, whenever we do anything, that act impacts the entirety of humankind. So, let's do something good, and let's do it now.

Don't wait to do something big. If the opportunity to do a big positive and helpful thing presents itself, then jump on it. In the meantime, don't wait to do something grand. Try a smile or a word of encouragement. Family and friends present prime opportunities for positive harmonious and unifying connection. Open yourself to sharing your thoughts, your observations, your hopes, your dreams, and even your doubts and fears. But don't limit these interactions to those with whom you feel closely attached. Remember that you're attached to all of humanity. Outside of your intimate circles are endless opportunities for meaningful connection. On a recent outing to the market, I retrieved an item from a high shelf for a person who was not quite tall enough to reach it. During this same shopping excursion, I dropped one of my grocery items on the floor, and another shopper bent down to pick it up for me. I could have picked it up myself, but with his kind gesture, the other shopper affirmed our connectedness.

I almost referred to this good Samaritan as a stranger. But

then I remembered this Will Rogers quote: "A stranger is just a friend that I haven't met yet." We are all companions on this pilgrimage to unity. Embrace your companions. None are strangers. Always keep in mind that what impacts one, impacts all. "Ask not for whom the bell tolls. It tolls for thee."

Where do we start? This innocent question often confounds us and freezes us where we stand. But once we realize that the place to start is where we are, we become empowered. We start by offering a smile to a person who might appear troubled. We tell a friend how important their support has been. We ask an elderly neighbor if they need any errands run. We help build homes for those in need. We look for value in someone else's difference. We share our humanity with our fellow humans. We start from where we are. We open ourselves to the bounty of our fellow humans.

Maya Angelou once said, "I have learned that every day you should reach out and touch someone. People love a warm hug, or just a friendly pat on the back."

CHAPTER 5

THE WEB OF LIFE

"All men die. But not all men really live."

—SIR WILLIAM WALLACE

"Every man must decide whether he will walk in the light of creative altruism or in the darkness of destructive selfishness."

—DR. MARTIN LUTHER KING JR.

When I am speaking about interdependence, I am not talking about altruism in the classic sense of purely unselfish concern for the welfare of others without concern for the benefit to oneself. I am talking about a recognition that the general welfare of others benefits and is in the self-interest of each of us. By enhancing the life experience of others, we automatically expand and enrich our own lives. In essence, promoting and contributing to the betterment of others may be the ultimate form of self-betterment.

In 2015 Sanyin Siang, Executive Director of Duke University's Leadership and Ethics Center at the Fuqua School of Business, wrote on creative altruism in a contributor's column of the HuffPost: "I look at the leaders and students with whom I engage, the most successful ones—those who have credibility and have the ability to influence others, are all creative altruists. Sometime in their journey, they've made a choice (whether deliberate or through formation of habit) that intentionally finding ways of helping others is non-negotiable."

In other words, we are each related parts of the undivided whole of humankind. Our strength and well-being are derived from our harmonious connectedness to this unity. I am a part of you, as opposed to apart from you, and part of everyone else who exists and those who have existed or who will exist. While my footprint is unique, it is unique only as a marker within humanity's march toward enlightened being. My uniqueness only has value if it facilitates others to optimize their uniqueness in the pursuit of the commonweal or general welfare of all.

Each of us is unique and gifted with something that only we can contribute to humanity. Dr. Benjamin Mays, former president of Morehouse University, said, "Every man and woman is born into the world to do something unique and something distinctive and if he or she does not do it, it will never be done." We each are gifted with a unique song to sing. The songs are not mine or yours but ours. The gifts of our songs are gifts to humankind. And we are blessed with the privilege and obligation to sing these songs to the world.

I was recently watching an episode of the very popular Netflix series *All American*. As they wrestle with whether or not to take a strong public position on a moral issue confronting the larger community, one of the main characters in the series says to his teammates, "This ain't about one of us. It's about all of us!"

We cannot sever ourselves from the whole. We can refuse to contribute our gifts, and we can delude ourselves into a sense of independence or superiority. But we are inescapably connected one to another. "This ain't about one of us. It's about all of us."

President John F. Kennedy famously said, "Ask not what your country can do for you. Ask what you can do for your country." I will take the liberty of expanding on this pronouncement by saying, "Ask not what humanity can do for you. Ask what you can do for humankind. By casting your good into the world, you strengthen the cosmos and consequently strengthen yourself."

We often seek to excuse bad behavior by falling back on the time-worn excuse that "nobody is perfect." We injure others, whether emotionally, physically, or fiscally, and attempt to expunge our fault by saying, "It was not my intent," or "I am sorry." Yet we knew before we inflicted the harm that what we were doing was at the expense of some other person or group. Because the other was not valued as we value ourselves, we felt perfectly comfortable in our actions. But when we harm another human being, we inevitably harm ourselves.

I know that if my actions and yours are focused on promoting the general welfare of society, your world and mine will benefit. I would be perfectly correct in saying that nobody is perfect. But everybody can be better. That is our goal. We can all be better.

In fact, to forsake egoism in pursuit of enriching this web of life may be the most profound and purest form of selfishness. If I seek to be whole, I must endeavor to make you whole. A better world for you means a better world for me. What impacts you impacts me. If I am seeking my own welfare, I must endeavor to enhance your welfare. What impacts one of us inevitably impacts all of us.

In order to achieve our goal of perfecting community, we must be self-actuating. We cannot wait for someone else to become better. We cannot say, "I will if they will." Each of us must follow the advice of Gandhi: "You must be the change you wish to see in the world."

One of my favorite stories vividly illustrates this essential component of human spiritual growth. A woman in India was upset that her son was eating too much sugar. Regardless of how often she counseled her son to reduce his sugar consumption, he persisted in yielding to his sweet tooth. Finally, the woman decided to take her son to see the son's hero—Mahatma Gandhi. Having been granted an audience with Gandhi, the mother approached the great man and humbly said, "Sir, my son eats too much sugar. It is not good for his health. Would you please advise him to stop eating it?" Gandhi turned to her son and said, "Go home and come back in two weeks." The woman, looking confused, took her son's hand and led him home. She was mystified that Gandhi had not admonished the boy to stop eating sugar.

Two weeks later, the mother returned to Gandhi with the boy in tow. Gandhi motioned for the boy to come forward. He looked the boy in the eye and said, "Boy, you should stop eating sugar. It is not good for your health." The boy looked adoringly at his idol and promised that he would stop eating sugar. The boy's mother turned to Mr. Gandhi in confusion and asked, "Why didn't you tell him that two weeks ago when I brought him here to see you?" Gandhi smiled at the mother and said, "Mother, two weeks ago I was still eating sugar myself."

I don't have all the answers to the profound and universal

questions of our purpose in the cosmos. But I am constantly questioning and seeking. I ask you to join me on this journey of discovery. I ask you to question those things that you have been programmed to accept as verities or absolutes. I believe that you will find, as I have, that sometimes the question is more important than the answer. Questioning reveals options and can be the key to unlocking a whole new world of possibility and promise.

Lao Tzu wrote in the *Tao Te Ching*, "We mold clay into a pot, but it is the emptiness inside that makes the vessel useful." We are all vessels to be filled.

Picture yourself as one uniquely shaped piece in a giant puzzle, surrounded by an infinity of other uniquely shaped puzzle pieces. Without you and your specific uniqueness, the puzzle cannot be completed. And you and your uniqueness are irrelevant without the rest of the puzzle. Just as pieces of a puzzle only have value as parts of the puzzle, we as individual human beings only have value in relationship to the whole of humanity.

For just a moment, imagine that you are a master gear maker. Using the finest materials and most precise measurements and engineering techniques, you have devised a method to build the fastest, most perfectly balanced, and strongest cogwheel in the world. Your cogwheel will revolve twice as fast as the next fastest cogwheel in existence.

But are you the most effective gear maker? The sole purpose of a cogwheel is to mesh with other cogwheels to drive a mechanism. For your cogwheel to play its systemic role effectively, it will have to moderate its rotational speed to synchronize with the rotational speeds of the other cogwheels. If it operates at its top, individually superior speed, which is at least twice as fast as the top speed of the other cogwheels, your cogwheel is useless and potentially destructive. Only if you can bring the other cogwheels up to the standard of your magnificent cogwheel can it make the mechanism better. Only if the entire mechanism is made better will your cogwheel realize its potential. Like our exceptional cogwheel, we only have value if we fit in with and help others to optimize the performance of the whole.

You must employ your individual uniqueness in a way that benefits the whole! All else is waste.

If I make no other impression in this treatise, I hope to impress upon you that it is not about you—but then again, it is. The truth is that it is not all about you. You exist as a part of a far vaster whole. In order to fully realize yourself, you must amalgamate yourself to the whole. You can start by doing something to help someone else every day. I must stress that by positively interacting with others every day, being better will become habitual. By committing to bettering the whole, you will begin to see yourself through others and will realize your uniqueness as an essential part of the whole. You will self-actualize in a way that allows you to reach your full potential. Therefore, even though it is not all about you, it is ultimately about you.

Our uniqueness as essential pieces of the whole is why we exist. We must continue to evolve as spiritual beings to complete the puzzle and, in so doing, complete ourselves.

It is why we must be better!

CHAPTER 6

WE ARE DROPS
IN THE OCEAN

"Accept the things to which fate binds you, and love the people with whom fate brings you together, but do so with all your heart."

—MARCUS AURELIUS

"You must not lose faith in humanity. Humanity is an ocean; if a few drops of the ocean are dirty, the ocean does not become dirty."

—MAHATMA GANDHI

On September 11, 2001, we witnessed the deadliest attack on America since Pearl Harbor. This event struck close to home for me and crystallized my thinking about our human interconnectedness.

At the time I was a managing director for a company that had about 1,900 employees working or visiting at our satellite offices in the World Trade Center Towers One and Two. My own office was on the forty-sixth floor of our Midtown Manhattan headquarters. At the south end of our hallway, there was a glass window wall with an unobstructed view of the World Trade Center buildings, which were located about three miles to the south. Along with several other employees, I stood at that window and watched in horror at the chaos taking place. At first we assumed that a small plane had gone off course and accidentally struck one of the towers. But our assumption was soon proved wrong when we witnessed the second plane deliberately fly into the second tower.

We lost 295 of our 1,900 Trade Center employees in the terrorist attack. I knew some of the people who died on that tragic day. One of them was a manager from one of our offices in Texas. He had flown in for a meeting that day. Another was a young woman with whom I had shared a taxi a few weeks earlier. The last time that I spoke with her, she was thrilled that she had just been promoted.

The United States government's response to this attack was to enter two seemingly endless military engagements in Afghanistan and Iraq. These two wars have resulted in tens of thousands of United States military casualties and far more innocent civilian casualties in Afghanistan and

Iraq. The conflict in Afghanistan continued for more than twenty years, with no visible benefit to any of the nations involved or to humanity writ large.

Why are we so hell-bent on burning the house in which we dwell? Why have we not learned that what harms one of us harms all of us? What do we gain through another's loss? And why is our automatic response to a harmful act an equal or greater retaliatory harm to humanity?

Is any war necessary, or are they merely manifestations reflecting our instinct to destroy what is perceived as different? We fear what is different. We hate what we fear. And we desire the destruction of what we hate.

Maybe, instead, we could flip this and learn to value, embrace, and incorporate our differences. Continuous, conscious, and reflexive application of love, caring, sharing, and support for all is how we will become whole as individuals and as humanity.

On our journey, we will encounter some who, for whatever reason, seek to oppose the good that others are striving to put into the world. It is our duty not only to stay on the path to wholeness but to confront those who would block the path. Evil and evildoers will always exist. Examples of them abound: Caligula, Hitler, Stalin, Idi Amin, Queen Mary I (Bloody Mary), and Irma Ida Grese (Beast of Belsen, a Nazi concentration camp) are infamous names we recognize and condemn. But there are also many examples of lesser-known evildoers.

One such individual is Alfried Krupp von Bohlen und Halbach, more commonly known as Alfried Krupp. Alfried was the son of Bertha Krupp who, at age sixteen, inherited the massive Friedrich Krupp manufacturing company, which was Germany's armorer for 400 years. The Krupps not only manufactured armaments for Germany; they also sold armaments to countries who were at war with Germany. Profit was the Krupp family driving force.

And they certainly were profitable. The Krupp mansion, named Villa Hugel, consisted of 269 air-conditioned rooms situated in a sixty-nine-acre park. Villa Hugel served as the primary Krupp family residence from 1873 through World War II. The Krupps's guests did not have to be concerned about intruding on the Krupps's privacy: in addition to the main house, the estate included a guest house, Kleines Haus (Little House), which consisted of sixty rooms.

During World War II, Alfried Krupp was sole proprietor of the Krupp manufacturing empire. Throughout the war, Alfried vastly increased his company's profits by employing slave labor to manufacture Germany's armaments. Alfried's slave labor was supplied by Hitler's Nazi government. Most of the laborers were Jewish prisoners from Nazi concentration camps. When the German military suggested that, for security reasons, more of the work be performed by free German laborers, Alfried insisted on continuing to use unpaid slave laborers. According to a Krupp employee, even when it was clear that the war was lost, Alfried kept 520 Jewish girls, many little more than children, working under brutal conditions. Following the war, Alfried was convicted of crimes against humanity at the Nuremberg Trials and sentenced to twelve years' imprisonment at Landsberg Prison. After only three years in prison, Alfried Krupp was pardoned and released on grounds that he was essential to the reconstruction of Germany. It appears that evil was pardoned.

Though those particular evildoers may have dwelled in the past, their spirits infest the present, and their modern-day acolytes will attempt to sow division today and into the future. Hate and division, if allowed to take root and flourish, become a cancer that eats away the healthy tissue of interconnected, harmonious human community. But they can only prevail if we give hate and division free rein. We cannot pardon evil. To stand by as a witness to evil and do nothing is to be complicit in that evil. Moral neutrality is not an option! Mahatma Gandhi and Dr. Martin Luther King Jr. chose the path of nonviolent confrontation and opposition to evil and were unwilling to bear silent witness to immoral and inhuman acts.

Oskar Schindler (about whom the movie *Schindler's List*

was based) was a German industrialist and member of the Nazi party. But Schindler, with the help of his wife Emilie, saved 1,200 of his Jewish workers during the Nazi extermination transport campaign. At grave personal risk, he gave succor to those humanity had abandoned. Emilie Schindler died in 2001. Her tombstone includes the words: *"Wer einen Menschen rettet, die Ganze Weldt* ("Whoever saves one life, saves the entire world"). Today, more than 8,500 descendants of those whose lives were saved by Oskar and Emilie Schindler are alive. One survivor stated that her grandchildren and great-grandchildren numbered more than 150.

Schindler was not a perfect person by far, but he made a heroic effort to be better and consequently he left us with a better world.

Lech Walesa, a shipyard electrician fed up with the human rights abuses in his home country of Poland, stood up and confronted the abusers. He organized the solidarity movement that confronted Poland's tyrannical, autocratic rule. In the process, Walesa was arrested numerous times and lost several jobs. He and his family were surveilled at home with hidden listening devices and were under constant physical threat. But his unwavering resolve inspired others to raise their own voices and join in his efforts, coordinating union strikes and eventually forcing free elections, the formation of a new government, and Poland's entry into the free-market economy. In 1983, Walesa was awarded the Nobel Peace Prize.

Nelson Mandela may be the ultimate symbol of one person's individual power to shape a better world. Practicing as a lawyer, Mandela was for many years a Black South African anti-apartheid freedom fighter. Mandela was appointed as president of the African Nationalist Congress party's Transvaal branch, which was actively working to overthrow the cruel restrictions of the Whites-only National Party government's apartheid system. In 1961, Mandela led a sabotage campaign against the government. This led to him being sentenced to life imprisonment in 1962. Mandela subsequently spent more than twenty-seven years in prison. Amid growing domestic and international pressure, he was eventually released from prison in 1990. For the next few years, he collaborated with the White South African president, F. W. de Klerk, to end apartheid. This collaboration eventually led to establishment of the 1994 multiracial general election, in which Mandela was elected president of the Republic of South Africa.

During his presidency, Mandela emphasized reconciliation between the country's racial groups. He understood that we win together, or we perish separately. Some observers on the right continued to view him as a left-wing terrorist, while many on the left felt that he was too eager to reconcile with apartheid supporters. But Mandela had a higher vision for a path to harmonious unity. He understood that none of us wins until all of us win. In 1993, he was awarded the Nobel Peace Prize for his visionary and symbiotic leadership.

Confucius stated, "Before you embark on a journey of revenge, dig two graves."

Often it only takes one person to stand up to evil for others of like mind to join in. When evil is encountered, we must stand and act, because to not act against evil is to be complicit in that evil. Our actions are not against the evildoers but against the evil that they do.

When you hear the words "silent majority," your alarm bells should chime. There is nothing silent in the silent majority. It is in the silence of the majority that evil takes root and thrives. Until the silent majority finds its voice and acts in the spirit of oneness, we cannot create a better and more harmonious world. And we cannot allow ourselves to be deterred by those who follow the path of harmful actions or rhetoric. Whether their actions are intentional or merely characteristic of their nature, we must confront them resolutely.

I believe that the evildoers will always be with us. Though Hitler may have died, his spirit lives on. We must struggle to unveil and neutralize the purveyors of evil wherever they show themselves. They are the cancer that seeks to block and destroy harmonic unity. And cancers must be excised before they metastasize. Most World War II-era Germans were not Nazis or even Nazi sympathizers. But too many turned a blind eye to the atrocities perpetrated by the Third Reich. This blind acceptance of inhuman acts and unbearable suffering of their fellow human beings also led to horrible postwar suffering for the entire nation.

I really started to envision a better world when I realized that my life was not just about me but about all of us. It was the realization that the world did not exist for me but that I existed for the world. It was the understanding that I was merely a vessel, created for the express purpose of adding my uniqueness to the great puzzle of humanity.

My life only has significance as a strand in life's web. It is my connection to the rest of humanity that gives my existence meaning. Our lives only have meaning when offered in service to others. Only when we are in harmonic pitch with the other strands in the web do our unique songs resonate with meaning.

We must stop focusing on who we are and explore why we are. We are all here to help each other fit our pieces into that great puzzle. We must consider how to make our songs resonate with the songs of others. When we open ourselves to the value in others and to other ways, we unlock the door to our truly authentic selves.

How we complete ourselves is fully dependent on our relationship, through other individuals, to the whole of humanity. There is a phenomenon that I have termed *intuitive coexistence.* I define this as a subliminal understanding that we are strands in the web of life and our well-being is dependent on facilitating the well-being of others. If we focus at all times on making others feel welcome, wanted, and important; if we make it our constant focus to ease the burdens of others; if we always seek we instead of me—then we will achieve intuitive coexistence.

I was witness to one of the most striking examples of intuitive coexistence on a business trip to Tokyo. I was exploring the shopping wonders of the Ginza area when I approached a major intersection with traffic lights on all four corners. I have since learned that this was the world-renowned Shibuya Crossing—you may have seen it in movies such as *Lost in Translation, The Fast and the Furious,* or *Tokyo Drift.* To my surprise, the pedestrian crossing signals on all four corners of the intersection lit up, at once stopping vehicle traffic in all directions. The intersection immediately became a scramble with as many as three thousand pedestrians simultaneously streaming in all directions. On its busiest days, it is estimated that as many as half a million pedestrians will use the Shibuya Crossing.

As amazing as this chaotic movement was to me, I found that this seemingly infinite crowd never bumped into or brushed up against one another. Amazing! How could they do that?

I attribute this seemingly surreal experience to the physical and cultural history of the country of Japan. Japan is an island nation with a large number of people living with limited land and personal space. Over the centuries, the Japanese have learned to live symbiotically with each other for the good of the whole. When you live in small dwellings with paper walls, you develop a sense for intuitive coexistence. The Tokyo-based architecture professor Julian Worrall has said the Shibuya Crossing is "a great example of what Tokyo does best when it's not trying."

But I have observed this phenomenon of community harmonization elsewhere. A couple of years ago I read about a college women's baseball team where two young women players carried the opposing team's injured player around the bases after she had hit a home run so that the home run would count. This was the winning run against their team in the conference championship. Let's record a win for humanity. We are a part of and not apart from the whole. Your win is my win.

More than 2,500 years ago, Confucius stated, "Life is really simple, but we insist on making it complicated." I firmly believe that the way to a better world is simple. In that vein I have attempted to make this book as simple as I could.

I know that we will be better simply because we wish to be better. We are no longer willing to be spectators in this great game of life. We will be actors. As Gandhi said, "You must be the change you wish to see in the world." I will not burden you with preachments. You already carry the answers to life's mystery if you are willing to ask the questions. If you simply observe the world around us, you will discover how your uniqueness can contribute to the benefit of the whole and therefore your own well-being and growth.

Like Shibuya Crossing, we can arrive at a point where we unconsciously conduct ourselves in ways that do not harm but enhance the lives of others. We are at that intersection, poised for a quantum leap into a brave new future of unlimited human innovation spurred by the novelty of symbiotic interactions. Our personal uniqueness, when blended with the uniqueness of others, creates possibilities for a more perfect you, a more perfect me, a more perfect us, and a more perfect world. Ask yourself: what have I done today that makes the world—my world, your world, and our world—a better world than it was yesterday?

Let us continue to challenge ourselves and others with that very simple question. The time is now.

James Baldwin said, "There is never a time in the future in which we will work out our salvation. The challenge is in the moment; the time is always now." All of us will find unparalleled fulfillment and celebration of life in seeking Interdependence Day.

As I stressed at the beginning of this treatise, I don't presume to teach. My goal is to facilitate your self-examination. I want to accompany you on your quest to discover and sing the unique song that is your gift to the world. I want us to bring harmonic resonance to the web of life.

CONCLUSION

The Power and Possibility of You, Me, and Us

"Trust yourself. Be the kind of self that you will be happy to live with all your life. Make the most of yourself by fanning the tiny, inner sparks of possibility into flames of achievement."

—GOLDA MEIR

I have written this book in order to share my philosophy of life bolstered by the wisdom of men and women who have, over the centuries, offered us a better way forward. I am thoroughly convinced that we are on the brink of an age of spiritual enlightenment, expanded consciousness, and the revelation of human interconnectedness.

The book is not about you—it is about all of us. It is about how our individual uniqueness and the uniqueness of others are essential elements to humanity's march toward oneness. Therefore, you do not need to abandon your uniqueness. Rather, you must employ your uniqueness in the service of others. Being of service to others does not make us servants. Instead, it immeasurably advances humanity.

And why is this interconnectedness important to you or to me? It is essential because we are parts of the whole, and as individuals, we can never be complete until the whole of humankind is complete and in harmonious accord. We must learn to embrace our oneness as the heart and lungs must employ their uniqueness in oxygenating and circulating the blood that nourishes the entire body. We cannot separate ourselves from the web of life. We are a part of— not apart from—that web.

We must not wait for someone else to take the first step to being better. We cannot wait for permission to be better. We cannot wait until it feels more comfortable to become better. We can begin now. We can begin from wherever we are. We can begin with something small or something large. We can begin with whoever or whatever is at hand. But we must begin. The time is now. As the famous Nike advertising slogan says, "Just do it."

The welfare of society is our welfare. When you hurt, I hurt. Anything that lessens you lessens me. Your joy is my joy. We can and must create a better world today.

Continuous, conscious application of love, caring, sharing, and supporting all others is the way.

In closing, I once more borrow from Leo Tolstoy. In his epic novel *War and Peace*, one of the characters says to his young protégé, "I would never be so bold as to say I know the truth. No one alone can attain truth; only stone upon stone, with the cooperation of all."

No one of us, neither me nor you, carries all the truth. But we each carry a small and essential part of that truth. Together we will complete the puzzle. We will find where our own uniqueness belongs in that universal truth. We will, via interdependent collaboration with others—whether one on one, in groups, in organizations, locally, nationally, or globally—find our unique place in the cosmos!

"Don't you know yet? It is your light that lights the world."

—RUMI

Now is our time to be more than we have been. Imagine!

ACKNOWLEDGEMENTS

I am forever grateful to those who said to me, "You should write a book."

Thirty years ago, my friend Barbara Byrd was the first person to tell me that I had something to say that needed to be said in a book. And, for years now my friends, George Clopton and Roy Bostic, have pressed me to share what I have shared with them on a more scalable platform than I could ever accomplish one on one or in my consulting and advisory engagements. So, thank you for believing in me.

My editors have been invaluable to me in this endeavor. I am fortunate to have several accomplished authors among my friends. Dr. Jeanne Porter King read the early version of my manuscript and pointed out some critical omissions and asked constructive questions. Likewise, Dr. Chiji Ohayia took the time to offer crucial editorial advice. And my literary muse, the late Quandra Prettyman Stadler Smith, Literature Professor, Barnard College of Columbia University, was not only kind enough to read my manuscript but also encouraged me when I encountered the inevitable writer's block.

My publisher's editor Chip Blake proved to be a fellow seeker as well as a committed editor. He made it abundantly clear that though I had written a good book, I could make it great. He understood my path and helped me to pursue it authentically. And I am indebted to the editorial group at the Foreign Policy Association for their insightful editorial review and comments. Without doubt I had the benefit of the best editorial support available.

So many have for so long contributed to my writing of this book. My wife Helen allowed me the time and space to pour myself into this project. And it is the love and support of Helen, our children and granddaughters that have kept me on track. Then there are the myriads of those who have come into my life and made me better. I will not attempt to name you all. It would require a list longer than my book. Some have been lifelong friends; others were co-workers or neighbors. Some came and went from my life so casually and quickly that it might be difficult to assess how they contributed to me becoming better. It may have been a server in a restaurant who said, "I appreciate your business."

Or it might have been a total stranger who smiled or spoke on the street. In fact, this past weekend Scott, a server in one of my favorite restaurants, made a point of telling our party, "I like you guys." Four words that made my day and will be a part of who I am going forward. Great or small, it is all good.

And I love you all and I am better for sharing this web of life with you.

Lightning Source UK Ltd.
Milton Keynes UK
UKHW011848231222
414411UK00013B/332/J